URBAN YOUTH SURVIVAL GUIDE

A MANUAL FOR OVERCOMING THE ODDS

I0459025

URBAN

YOUTH JUSTICE

DR. PEDRO RODRIGUEZ

Mission: To Proclaim Transformation and Truth
Publisher: Transformed Publishing, Cocoa, FL
Website: www.transformedpublishing.com
Email: transformedpublishing@gmail.com

ISBN: 978-1-953241-79-5

URBAN YOUTH SURVIVAL GUIDE

A MANUAL FOR OVERCOMING THE ODDS

PROSPECT ST

NARROW ROAD

FAITH

PURPOSE

NO HOPE

DR. PEDRO RODRIGUEZ

Endorsements

Pedro is a seasoned expert in the Juvenile Justice field, bringing both personal experience and deep passion to his work with urban youth. Having overcome significant challenges himself, he now dedicates his life to giving back. This survival guide is a powerful, practical resource that helps young people understand how they arrived at their current circumstances—and more importantly, how they can begin the journey toward healing and restoration. This curriculum has the potential to create real, lasting change and break generational cycles.

-Tommy "Urban D." Kyllonen
Lead Pastor, Author, Artist

Pedro's commitment to authenticity and his passion for uplifting others shines through on every page. I wholeheartedly recommend this book to anyone ready to be challenged and inspired to embrace new opportunities and pursue their fullest potential.

-Sammy Ortiz
Founder/CEO Y- E- S
(Young Entrepreneurial Students)
Pastor | Social Entrepreneur | US Army Veteran

After having worked with justice-involved young people for nearly 40 years, I can say with confidence that this Survival Guide truly contains everything one needs for overcoming all the odds stacked against those who end up in the justice system. And it comes from a trusted coach who has been there. I've known Pedro for nearly 20 years and have watched him navigate some of the toughest things one could face. Not just from childhood, but throughout his adult life as well. In these pages Pedro opens his life and freely gives lessons he has come by the hard way. Not in a preaching kind of way, but in a way you would hope a loving parent would give. Thank you for this gift Pedro. You've never forgotten where you've come from, and you are always looking out for others who are traveling some of the same paths you have known so well.

-Scott Larson
Founder, Straight Ahead Ministries
Worcester, MA

Dr. Pedro Rodriguez's *Urban Youth Survival Guide* is more than just a book—it's a testament to turning pain into purpose. Having overcome the odds himself and worked with thousands of young people involved in the juvenile justice system in Florida and beyond, Dr. Rodriguez offers a powerful, heartfelt roadmap. This guide will inspire any young person seeking hope and a sense of direction, proving that no matter the circumstances, there's always a way to find purpose and move forward.

-Eugene Schneeberg
Director
Every Youth Every Facility

Dr. Rodriguez has written this book from a wealth of personal experience and academic study. His passion for urban youth shines through each and every page. Subtitled, *A Manual for Overcoming the Odds*, this book delivers on its promise to equip troubled youth to break the cycle of street life. The book is practical, including thoughtful and wise reflection questions and action steps. Above all, Dr. Rodriguez understands that the only viable solution to all of life's problems is founded on the person and work of Jesus Christ.

-Chad Tvenstrup
Lead Pastor
Christ Presbyterian Church
Bradenton, FL

Acknowledgments

First and foremost, I give all glory and honor to God, who saw me not as I was, but as I could be. Without His grace and transforming power, there would be no story to tell and no book to write.

To my wife, Gedy, who believed in me when I was still learning to believe in myself—your love and patience have been the earthly reflection of God's faithfulness in my life.

To my children, who have forgiven my early failures and given me the chance to be the father I never had—your resilience inspires me daily.

To the countless mentors, pastors, and spiritual fathers who invested in me when I had nothing to offer in return—you exemplified the love that transforms lives.

To the young men and women I've had the privilege of mentoring—your courage to change keeps me pushing forward in my own journey.

To my editor and publishing team, who helped shape these raw experiences into a message of hope—thank you for believing in the power of this story.

And finally, to every reader holding this book—especially those who see themselves in these pages—know that your disadvantage is not your destiny. Your past is not your future. Your struggles are not your identity.

Your story is still being written, and the best chapters lie ahead.

A Note to Readers

This book uses direct language and real experiences to connect with those facing similar challenges. While some content may be intense, it reflects the reality many urban youth face daily. The goal is not to glorify the struggles but to show a path through them.

Each chapter includes:

- Personal stories from my journey.
- Practical tools for your situation.
- Biblical principles for guidance.
- Action steps for moving forward.
- Questions for reflection.

Use this book as both a manual and a mirror—a way to see where you are and a map to where you want to be.

How to Use This Book

1. Read each chapter thoroughly.
2. Complete the reflection questions.
3. Try the suggested action steps.
4. Return to relevant sections as needed.
5. Share your insights with others on the same journey.

Remember: This isn't just a book to read—it's a tool for transformation.

URBAN YOUTH SURVIVAL GUIDE

A MANUAL FOR OVERCOMING THE ODDS

Table of Contents

Introduction: Breaking the Cycle

This isn't just another book. It's a survival guide—a manual written in the language of the streets but carrying the wisdom of heaven. I'm writing this because I've walked the path many of you are on right now. Born in 1976 to a 15-year-old mother and 16-year-old father in the rough neighborhoods of Jersey City, New Jersey, I learned early that life doesn't hand out easy passes.

From the start, the odds were stacked against us. My teenage parents, struggling with poverty, could barely find jobs. My grandparents had to step in to help raise me. And though I had moments of normal childhood—playing games, running the streets, being a kid—the cracks in our foundation started showing early. My father battled his addictions. I remember nights spent in my mother's car, searching local bars, being sent inside at a young age to look for him. The dysfunction, the arguments, the instability—it was all there, teaching me lessons I never should have had to learn.

Then came the phone call that changed everything. I was 12, ironing my shirt for school—already learning to fend for myself—when my mother got the news. My father had passed away, his liver destroyed by the substances that had controlled his life. My mother, broken by grief, turned to drugs to numb her pain. And just like that, I became another statistic: a fatherless child in an urban jungle.

But this book isn't just my story. It's a roadmap for every young person growing up in broken homes, navigating life without father figures, trying to find their way through the urban battlefield. I'm writing to you—yes, you—who might be:

- Growing up without a father's guidance.
- Living in survival mode.
- Making choices that seem right in the moment but lead to destruction.
- Facing the school-to-prison pipeline.

- Battling with drugs and alcohol.
- Dealing with early parenthood.
- Struggling to find your true identity.
- Fighting to overcome the trauma of your past.

I've been there. By 16, I was a high school drop-out with criminal charges. By 19, I was a father to two daughters from different mothers. I've worn the ankle monitor, done the work release, faced the parole officer. I've chased every empty promise the streets had to offer—money, women, drugs, status—thinking they could fill the void my father's absence left behind.

But here's what I discovered: nothing this world offers can fill that father-shaped hole in your soul. Not the dollar bills. Not the street cred. Not the relationships. Not the substances. Not the expensive clothes or the fancy cars or the temporary highs. These are all traps—paths that lead to early graves or prison cells.

At 21, I found something different. Something real. Through an encounter with Christ, I discovered my true identity and purpose. Seven months after giving my life to God, I married my first daughter's mother, Gedy. The transformation was so complete that today, at 48, I hold three college degrees—a long way from that high school dropout I used to be.

In these pages, you'll find:

- Practical tools for navigating life's challenges.
- Spiritual principles that can transform your reality.
- Real talk about overcoming odds that seem impossible.
- Stories that speak your language, not church talk.
- Strategies for breaking generational cycles.
- Ways to build resilience and overcome trauma.
- Hope for a future you might not yet be able to see.

We'll talk about everything—from dealing with a criminal record when trying to find work, to healing broken relationships, to finding your purpose in life. I'm not going to sugarcoat anything. We'll address the real issues: the anger, the pain, the confusion, the temptations, and the hard choices you face every day.

This book is designed to be your guide through:

- Overcoming the disadvantages of growing up fatherless.
- Breaking free from destructive patterns.
- Finding stability in an unstable world.
- Building a future despite your past.
- Discovering your true identity.
- Walking in faith when everything seems hopeless.

Each chapter combines my story with practical wisdom, street smarts with spiritual insight, real talk with real solutions. You'll find tools you can use today and principles that can guide you for a lifetime.

Remember this: your current situation is not your final destination. The statistics don't have to define you. The cycles can be broken. The patterns can be changed. The wounds can be healed.

Don't let anyone tell you what you can't become. Your past is just preparation for your purpose.

I'm living proof that God can transform a life completely—taking a broken, angry, lost young man from the streets and turning him into someone who can help others find their way. This book is part of that transformation, a tool to help you avoid the traps I fell into and find the purpose God created you for. Are you ready to break the cycle? Let's begin this journey together.

Chapter 1: The Disadvantage

From birth, I lacked stability. Life was complicated. The cycle of poverty set to repeat again. That's what the statistics say. Two kids trying to raise a kid, struggling to find work, both coming from poverty themselves. Our neighborhood wasn't the kind of place where dreams came easy.

My grandparents stepped in early, caring for me until my parents were old enough to stand on their own feet. Eventually, we got our own place, but that's when I began to see the reality of our situation. My father's addictions became the elephant in the room, growing larger and more destructive with each passing day.

Early Memories

I remember the nights clearly—too clearly. My father coming home late, alcohol on his breath.

My mother, desperate and worried, would pile me into the car to search the local bars. Picture this: a young boy, walking into smoky bars, searching for his father's face among the crowd. Those moments planted seeds of dysfunction that would grow wild in later years.

Life wasn't all darkness though. During the day, I was just a regular kid in Jersey City. I played tag, manhunt, wiffle ball, and kickball. My grades were good—straight A's even. From the outside, you might have called it a normal childhood.

The Night Everything Changed

Since the age of 12, etched in my mind, I have recounted the look on my mom's red tear-stained face when she returned home hours after receiving the phone call telling her my dad was dead. My father had been missing for a day and a half. The last time I'd seen him was Father's Day weekend.

They found his body later. His liver had exploded, and the autopsy revealed various substances in his system. I never expected to join the ranks of the fatherless.

The Spiral

That's when I first heard the lies—the whispers that would shape my future. Growing up in the neighborhood without a father meant I was destined to be another statistic. Maybe I believed those lies. Maybe I let them guide me down the wrong path. My straight A's plummeted to F's. I got expelled. My mother, already dealing with her own grief, had to watch her son spiral out of control.

The timeline of my decline was swift:

- Age 13: First arrest for shoplifting at the mall.
- Started smoking weed with cousins.
- Early exposure to explicit material found in my father's things.
- Sexual experimentation at a young age.

My mother tried to hold things together, working to pay the bills, but her own battles with addiction made consistency impossible. Soon we lost our place, and I moved back in with my grandparents—into a new neighborhood that introduced me to new friends and new troubles. We formed crews that operated like gangs. We cut class, chased girls, and found creative but illegal ways to make money.

The Void

The emotional and psychological effects were profound. Anger. Hurt. Confusion. These became my constant companions. The questions haunted me:

- Who would teach me how to be a man?
- How would I learn to be a father when I'd lost my own?
- What does it mean to be a husband?
- How do you treat a woman right?

Without answers, I turned to the streets for guidance. They turned me into something else entirely—a monster, as I'd later realize. My pursuit of happiness became nothing more than chasing material things, collecting conquests, pursuing what they now call "the bag."

I wasn't thinking about the future or setting goals. Living for the moment was hard enough. The streets had their own curriculum, and I was an eager student learning all the wrong lessons.

The disadvantage isn't just about what you're missing—it's about what fills that space instead.

Looking back now, I can see how each missing piece of guidance, each absent lesson about manhood and responsibility, created a vacuum that the streets were all too happy to fill. But understanding your disadvantage is the first step toward overcoming it. And that's what this chapter—this entire book—is about: recognizing where you start doesn't have to determine where you finish.

Reflection Questions

1. What are some significant childhood events that shifted the trajectory of your life (good or bad)?
2. What 'missing pieces' have affected your overall peace?
3. What misconceptions have you had to overcome?

Action Steps

1. Make a list of people who you are grateful to have crossed your path and why.
2. Write a letter of encouragement to your childhood self.

Journal Space

_____

_____

_____

_____

_____

_____

Chapter 2: He Bought the Lie

 The thief comes only to steal and kill and destroy; I have come that they may have life, and have it to the full.

-John 10:10

The lies start small. They whisper in your ear, settle in your mind, and before you know it, they're directing your whole life. I know because I bought into them all. Every single one.

The Lies I Believed

They told me a man was defined by:

- How many women he could possess.
- How much money he could earn.
- What material things he owned.
- His reputation on the streets.

These weren't just ideas—they became my identity. I attached myself to these lies like they were truth, pursuing them at all costs. But here's what those lies don't tell you: they leave you empty, broken, and at risk in ways you can't imagine until it's too late.

The Family Context

Even within my own family, these lies were reinforced. I was taught that manhood was about possession—of money, of things, of women. The streets only amplified these messages. We turned it into competition: who could get the most phone numbers at clubs, who could sleep with the most women, who could flash the most cash.

And then there were the darker lies—the ones that tried to write my story before I lived it. They said I wouldn't amount to anything, that I was just another brown boy destined for prison or death. Another statistic in the making.

The World's Definition vs. God's Truth

The world defines a man one way, but Scripture paints a completely different picture. According to God's word, a true man is:

- Humble
- Loving
- Caring
- A leader
- A father figure
- Someone who denies himself and carries his cross

John 10:10 reveals the stark contrast: while the enemy comes to kill, steal, and destroy, God offers us abundant life through Jesus. In that life—not in the lies—is where we find our:

- True identity
- Purpose
- Calling
- Peace

The Cost of the Lies

The world, our friends, even our family sometimes—they'll tell us it's okay to chase these empty pursuits. But by the time we realize the truth, we've often paid a heavy price:

- Lost freedom
- Broken relationships
- Wasted years
- Permanent consequences

I learned this the hard way. Having money, fame, power, and women made me feel like somebody. But that somebody wasn't me—it was a character I was playing in a story that always ends the same way: either dead or in prison.

The Reality Check

Let me paint you a picture of where these lies can lead you. Imagine:

- Wearing prison uniforms and slides.
- Being told when to shower.
- Being told when to use the restroom.
- Being told when to eat.
- Being told when to wake up.
- Being told when you can make a phone call.

In that cell, all those material possessions you fought for, worked for, or sold drugs for mean nothing. The fantasy of being some *Tony Montana*-type figure crashes hard against the concrete walls of reality.

Breaking Free from the Lies

Today, I challenge you to examine your own life. Don't let society's norms define you. Don't let culture describe who you are. The path of lies might seem attractive, but it leads to pain that sometimes has no turning back. Even if by God's grace you survive the struggle, some consequences you'll carry forever.

A Warning and a Promise

The lies start in your mind, travel to your heart, and then manifest in your actions. I thought stealing would make me somebody. I thought money would give me power. For a while, it did—until it almost took everything from me.

Remember this: material things aren't worth your freedom. That fake power isn't worth your life. Be careful what lie you buy, because the price tag might be higher than you can afford to pay.

But there's good news: in Christ, you can find:

- Healing
- Restoration
- Reconciliation
- True joy
- Lasting peace
- A life of impact

The choice is yours. Which story will you believe?

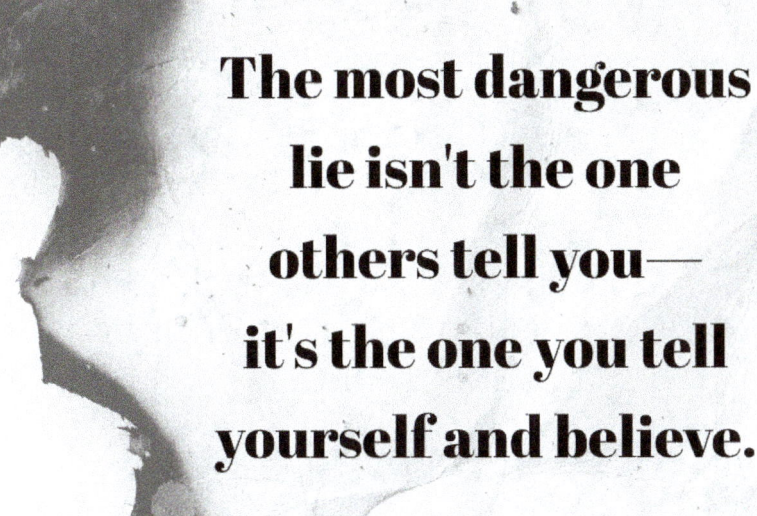

The most dangerous lie isn't the one others tell you— it's the one you tell yourself and believe.

Reflection Questions

1. What lies have you been told?
2. What messages from music, TV, and social media are shaping your choices?
3. Are the things you're pursuing truly satisfying you?
4. Are these pursuits distracting you from your real goals?
5. What setbacks have you experienced chasing these lies?

Action Steps

1. The purpose of lies are to distort and manipulate truth. Identify the truth the enemy does not / did not want you to discover.
2. Identify areas in your thinking that are hindering you from experiencing all you desire in Christ.

Journal Space

_____

_____

_____

_____

_____

_____

_____

_____

_____

_____

_____

_____

_____

_____

_____

_____

_____

_____

_____

_____

_____

_____

_____

_____

_____

_____

_____

_____

_____

_____

_____

_____

_____

_____

_____

_____

_____

Chapter 3: How It All Started

 Do not be misled: "Bad company corrupts good character."
— 1 Corinthians 15:33

The Weight of Early Choices

It starts so quietly, doesn't it? That first moment when you realize:

- Your parents aren't providing what you need.
- You feel abandoned and neglected.
- Life is forcing decisions on you too soon.
- You're carrying weights you're not ready to bear.

Suddenly, you're forced to be a man when you're still just a boy. No guidance. No wisdom. Just the pressure of survival pressing down on shoulders too young to carry such loads.

The First Steps Down

The path starts to look clearer when you see others who seem to have it figured out:

- They've got money in their pockets.
- They're having fun.
- They seem free from worry.
- They appear to have what you lack.

And there you are—not ready, not financially able, but so tempted. The first crime seems small, almost harmless. You get away with it once, twice, three times. Each success makes the next one easier, until breaking the law stops feeling like breaking anything at all.

The Numbing Process

Then comes the substances:

- A little sip here.
- A small puff there.
- Just trying this.
- Just experimenting with that.

Nobody ever tells you the whole truth:

- That one bad trip could destroy your mind forever.
- That crack rock could own your soul.
- That pipe could become your master.
- That bottle could wreck your family.
- That DUI could end your freedom.

The Fall

The descent happens so gradually:

- Your grades start dropping.
- Blackouts become normal.
- Your life starts falling apart.
- One compromise leads to another.
- What was wrong becomes right.
- Your conscience grows quiet.

Until one day, you're doing things you never imagined you'd do, living a life you never thought would be yours.

What They Never Tell You

They don't mention the consequences:

- That cell where others control your every move.
- Those early graves that claim the young.
- The way addiction steals your choices.
- How one decision can change everything forever.

Some consequences we can weather temporarily. Others? They reshape our entire future, leaving scars that never fade.

The Circle of Influence

 Walk with the wise and become wise, for a companion of fools suffers harm.

-Proverbs 13:20

Your circle changes you. It's that simple. Who you run with shapes:

- What you think is possible.
- What you consider normal.
- What you're willing to do.
- Who you become.

The Path to Destruction

It's a progression:

- Small compromises
- Bigger risks
- Seared conscience
- Lost values
- Forgotten morals
- Abandoned dreams

Maybe you remember:

- Going to church with your grandparents
- Having structure in your life
- Following certain values
- Knowing right from wrong

But somewhere along the way, you lost touch with all that.

The Mirror Moment

Stop. Right now. Look at where you are:

- What decisions led you here?
- How far have you drifted from what you knew was right?
- What consequences are you already facing?
- How could different choices have led to different outcomes?

The Truth About Success

Success isn't a straight line. It's built on:

- Discipline
- Consistent good choices
- Refusing to compromise
- Learning from mistakes
- Building positive habits

Without discipline, life becomes reckless—a series of failures stacked on failures. But with discipline, with good decisions stacked on good decisions, you can build something different.

Your Turning Point

Every choice you make today is:

- A brick in your future.
- A step toward or away from your goals.
- A vote for who you'll become.
- A seed that will bear fruit.

You can have everything you want in life, but:

- One bad decision can take it all away.
- Or a series of poor choices can keep it forever out of reach.

The Choice Is Yours

Start today:

- Make one good decision.
- Then another.
- Then another.

- Let discipline become your lifestyle.
- Let wisdom guide your steps.

Remember: The ride might not be what you want right now, but the destination is worth the discipline it takes to get there.

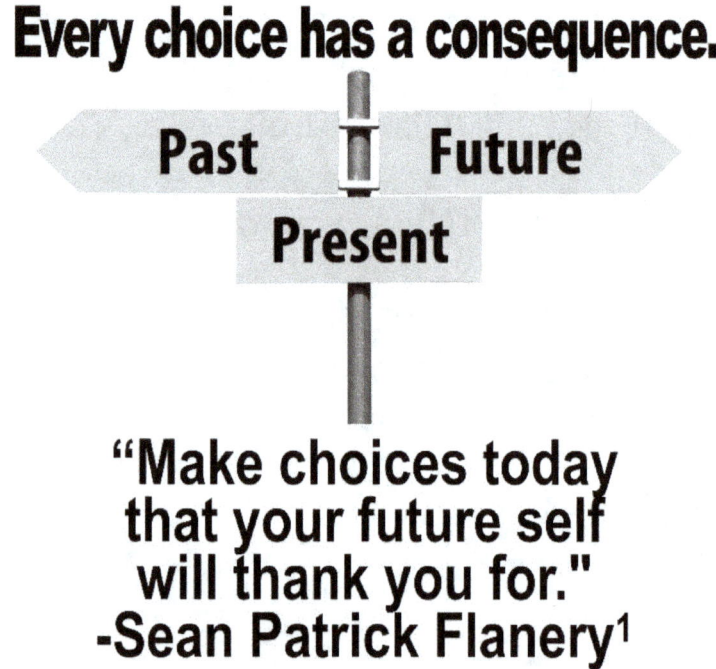

Every choice has a consequence.

Past   **Future**

Present

"Make choices today that your future self will thank you for."
-Sean Patrick Flanery[1]

[1]Cassandra. "Do Something Today That Your Future Self Will Thank You For." Joyful through It All, 14 Feb. 2022, www.joyfulthroughitall.com/do-something-today-that-your-future-self-will-thank-you-for/. Accessed 17 Sept. 2025.

Reflection Questions

1. What small decisions are you making today that could have big consequences tomorrow?
2. Who in your circle is pulling you up, and who is pulling you down?
3. What values or morals have you compromised that you need to reclaim?
4. How can you start building discipline in your life today?
5. What's one good decision you can make right now?

Action Steps

1. Write down three compromises you've made recently and their consequences.
2. Identify one positive influence in your life and strengthen that relationship.
3. Create a morning routine that starts your day with purpose.
4. Make a list of your non-negotiable values.
5. Choose one area of your life to apply strict discipline for the next 30 days.

Journal Space

_____
_____
_____
_____
_____
_____
_____
_____
_____
_____
_____
_____
_____
_____
_____
_____
_____
_____
_____
_____
_____
_____
_____
_____

Chapter 4: Conforming Patterns

The Search for Belonging

When you lose your father and your mother disappears into addiction, the world becomes a very lonely place. As a young Hispanic boy in a rough neighborhood, I found myself asking that universal question: *Where do I belong?*

The answer seemed to be waiting on every corner—with the "cool kids," the ones:

- Making money on the block
- Smoking weed
- Drinking
- Seeming to have it all figured out

The neighborhood's curriculum was clear and unforgiving:

- Dress this way
- Talk that way
- Chase women
- Collect "experiences"
- Build a reputation

And God forbid you didn't conform. The consequences were immediate: marked, excommunicated, treated as less than, mocked, bullied. In a world where belonging feels like oxygen, these were threats you couldn't ignore.

Conforming to Destruction

The pattern starts small:

- Getting in trouble at home
- Problems in the neighborhood
- First arrest
- Legal charges

But here's what they don't tell you about conformity: these destructive behaviors don't just stay behaviors—they become habits. And habits? They become chains.

Identity Theft

The saddest part isn't even the trouble you get into—it's losing yourself in the process. When you lose your identity, you become an empty vessel waiting to be filled by whatever label others put on you:

- Gangster
- Thug
- Gangbanger
- Addict
- Whatever they say you should be

And once you embrace that label, it owns you. It controls:

- Your thoughts
- Your feelings
- Your experiences
- Your future

The Cycles of Destruction

These unhealthy circles of influence lead to unhealthy cycles of life. It's a vicious spiral that keeps spinning:

The External Cycle:

- Fall into bad company
- Make poor choices
- Face consequences
- Seek comfort in the same crowd
- Repeat

The Internal Cycle:

- Feel frustrated
- Experience failure
- Can't face your own thoughts
- Grow angry
- Blame others
- Care less about the future

The Blame Game

You start carrying a chip on your shoulder:

- "My father wasn't there."
- "My mom is on drugs."
- "Where was everyone when I needed them?"

The anger becomes a constant companion, and the future? It shrinks to just getting through the moment.

The False Fillers

We try to fill the void with:

- Substances to numb the pain
- Casual relationships
- Expensive clothing
- Cars
- Jewelry
- Status
- Power

But here's the truth I learned the hard way: that void is specific. It's shaped for something—Someone—specific. You can pile all the world's treasures into it, but they'll just rattle around in that emptiness.

The Mirror Moment

I know because I had it all—everything the streets said would make me somebody. But every morning, I'd look in the mirror and see a stranger. Something was still missing. The hunger never went away. Deep down, a voice kept whispering: "This can't be it. This isn't all life is meant to be."

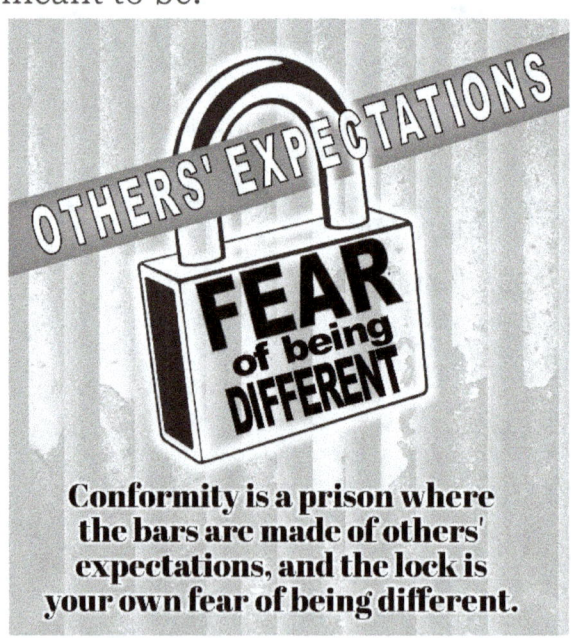

Reflection Questions

1. What patterns am I conforming to?
2. Who am I trying to please?
3. What void am I trying to fill?
4. Can I recognize myself in the mirror?
5. What's the real cost of belonging?

Action Steps

Remember: The path everyone else is walking isn't necessarily going somewhere you want to be. Visualize your ideal destination and outline the course to obtain it.

Journal Space

_____

_____

_____

_____

_____

_____

_____

_____

_____

_____

_____

_____

_____

_____

_____

_____

_____

_____

_____

_____

_____

_____

_____

_____

_____

_____

_____

_____

_____

_____

_____

_____

_____

_____

Chapter 5: The Chase

The Empty Pursuit

When you're a teenager with a father in the grave and a mother lost to drugs, the world becomes a maze where every path promises an escape. They call it "chasing the bag" now—the relentless pursuit of money, status, and temporary pleasure. But I call it what it really is: running from pain.

The Progression

The chase always starts small:

- A little weed to numb the pain.
- Selling it at school to make quick money.
- Expensive clothes to look the part.
- Jewelry to flash your status.
- Cars to prove your worth.

But here's what they don't tell you about the chase—it's like trying to fill a bucket with a hole in the bottom. The more you pour in, the faster it drains.

The False Validation

We created a scoreboard that measured manhood by all the wrong metrics:

- How many phone numbers you collected at the club.
- How many women you'd been with.
- How much you could spend in one night.
- What brands you wore.
- What car you drove.

It was all a competition, a desperate game of approval-seeking. If you didn't have these things, you were labeled:

- Broke
- A joke
- Not worth friendship
- Not cool enough to hang with

Deception

The shift happens so gradually you barely notice:

- Weed becomes your daily escape.
- Bottles of Hennessy become your weekend ritual.
- One-night stands become your measure of worth.
- Material possessions become your identity.

It's all "fun and games" until you realize you're trapped in what we call "temporary fulfillment with inevitable crash."

The True Cost

The destruction comes in waves:

- Physical deterioration
- Mental confusion
- Emotional numbness
- Spiritual death

You wake up one day and realize:

- You can't function without being high.
- Your worth is tied to your conquests.
- Your identity is wrapped in brands.
- Your soul is drowning in emptiness.

The Vicious Cycle

This lifestyle doesn't just hurt you—it turns you into someone who hurts others. It's a cycle of destruction that spreads:

- Pain creates more pain.
- Hurt people hurt people.
- Broken spirits break others.

The Statistics

Let me be brutally honest: the odds are stacked against anyone trying to "beat the game." I've yet to see someone truly win at this lifestyle. What I have seen:

- Friends lost to violence.
- Relatives consumed by addiction.
- Lives destroyed by pride.
- Decades wasted in prison cells.
- Teenagers dying over street credit.
- Families torn apart by choices that can't be undone.

The Real Void

That emptiness you're trying to fill? It has a purpose. That void is shaped for something specific—someone specific. It's meant for a relationship with Christ, the creator. Only then do you discover:

- True joy replaces temporary pleasure.
- Real peace defeats artificial highs.
- Authentic identity overcomes false status.
- Divine purpose trumps worldly pursuit.

The Transformation

When we accept Christ's influence in our lives, everything changes:

- Your mind gets renewed.
- Your heart is made new.
- Your feet find solid ground.
- Your steps gain direction.
- Your purpose becomes clear.

The things you once chased become the things you run from. The pleasures you once craved become the chains you break.

A Warning and a Choice

To every young man and woman reading this: be careful what you're chasing. Your pursuit will lead you to one of two destinations:

Option 1: A place of destruction.
- Early death
- Prison cell
- Rehab center
- Broken relationships
- Lost years
- Endless regret

Option 2: A place of purpose.

- ○ True identity
- ○ Lasting peace
- ○ Real relationships
- ○ Meaningful impact
- ○ Eternal significance
- ○ Divine fulfillment

The choice is yours, but remember: what you chase today determines where you'll stand tomorrow.

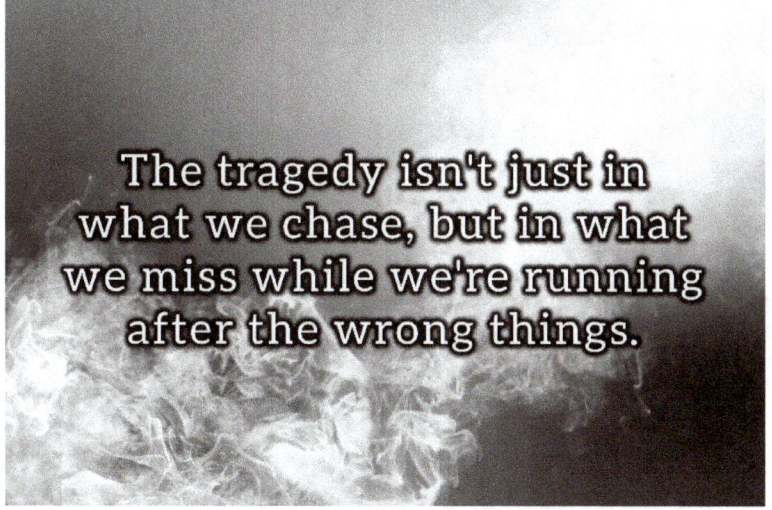

The tragedy isn't just in what we chase, but in what we miss while we're running after the wrong things.

Reflection Questions

1. What am I really running from?
2. What void am I trying to fill?
3. Is my pursuit leading me toward destruction or purpose?
4. What's the real cost of my current chase?
5. Am I ready to pursue something greater?

Action Steps

Remember: It's never too late to change what you're chasing, but for some, tomorrow might be too late to make that choice. Journal your response to this statement.

Journal Space

_____

_____

_____

_____

_____

_____

_____

Dr. Pedro Rodriguez

Chapter 6: Breaking Free

The Moment of Truth

Like in any chase, you eventually hit a wall. You get tired. Exhausted. After pursuing money, women, power, fame—all the things you thought would fill the void—you finally realize you've been lied to. The destructive patterns you've developed have formed addictive cycles, and breaking free seems impossible.

In this constant pursuit of trying to be happy, trying to fit in, trying to become somebody you were never created to be, you've:

- Developed bad habits.
- Hurt people around you.
- Hurt yourself.
- Become emotionally, mentally, spiritually, and physically drained.

And deep inside, all you want is to be free.

The Fear of Freedom

I've spoken to many youth leaving juvenile facilities after serving their time. When I ask if they're excited to go home, many respond with fear: "I'm afraid. I don't know if I'm ready. I don't want to fall back into these traps. All I know is stealing, getting high, and gang banging."

I remember being that young boy myself, sick and tired of the life I was living. I knew these pleasures were temporary. They weren't filling the void. After sobering up, after getting the things I wanted, I still craved more. I wanted freedom, but I didn't know what that looked like. I wondered: *Is change even possible?*

The Turning Point

My freedom began with a Bible—almost like a prescription handed to me by a pastor. At first, I rejected it: "Nah, I don't want that. That ain't for me." I let it sit in my home, untouched.

But something kept tugging at me. I picked up that book and began to read, not just the highlighted verses but beyond them. What happened next was history:

- My eyes opened.
- My mind shifted.
- My heart changed.
- I was transformed and empowered by God.

I found myself driven away from the things I once loved. The addictive cycles began to break. For the first time, I started to feel free:

- The hatred melted away.
- Unforgiveness lifted.
- Pain began to heal.
- I was being restored.

Building a New Life

I let go of old habits and developed new ones:

- Reading
- Praying

- Surrounding myself with the right people
- Building a real support system

No more hanging with jokers and clowns who only wanted me to follow them into their mess. *Sound familiar?*

The Process of Resilience

You're going to face disadvantages, obstacles, challenges, temptations, and trials in life. But these hardships build resilience. Scripture tells us that suffering produces godly character, endurance, and perseverance. These challenges either make you or break you.

But here's the truth: freedom is attainable. In Christ, those chains from past sinful desires break. We become new creations, craving new things as God begins a new work in us. We can stand tall with our heads held high, knowing we are His sons and daughters. He has a plan and purpose for us.

So walk in that freedom, young man. Walk in that freedom, young lady. He wants to empower and equip you to do greater things than you've ever imagined.

True freedom isn't doing whatever you want— it's becoming who you were created to be.

Reflection Questions

1. What addictive cycles are you struggling to break free from?
2. What's one step you can take today toward freedom?
3. Who can become part of your support system?
4. What new habits could replace your old destructive ones?
5. How might your story of breaking free inspire others?

Action Steps

1. Identify your main struggle and name it specifically.
2. Find one person you can be honest with about your struggles.
3. Create a daily routine that includes time for spiritual growth.
4. Remove one negative influence from your life this week.
5. Write down what freedom would look like for you.

Journal Space

Chapter 7: The Power of Faith

Do not conform to the pattern of this world, but be transformed by the renewing of your mind. Then you will be able to test and approve what God's will is—his good, pleasing and perfect will.

— Romans 12:2

Spiritual Transformation

As we utilize the gift of faith, as God sets us free, we undergo what's called spiritual transformation. That faith rises us up from the grave—it's like new breath to our dry bones. We go from spiritual death to life, from darkness to marvelous light.

Our minds are renewed. My favorite Scripture, Romans 12:2, tells us: "Do not conform to the pattern of this world". Don't be like everybody else. Instead, "Be transformed by the renewing of your mind." Then, the Scripture says, you will know His pleasing and perfect will.

Many of us have probably asked:

- What is God's will for my life?
- What is His purpose?
- Why am I here?

The answer comes through the renewing of your mind—spending time in God's Word, walking by faith, denying the things of the flesh.

The Unique Power of Faith

Faith is a beautiful, powerful thing. It helps us recover. It restores our relationship with God because Christ made it possible. No other religion offers you open access to God—the mediator, the bridge, the Redeemer who gives you life and relationship with the Father.

If you look for strength in yourself, you're limited. But in God, it's beyond you—it's unlimited. I love how the Scripture says, "The joy of the Lord is your strength" (*see* Nehemiah

8:10). Seek that joy that only He can give you. You'll never find joy or peace in Aisle 12 or Aisle 10 at your local retail store. It's only a gift from God.

The Power of Community

I had to cut off a lot of friends. God gave me new ones. What we call "hanging out" in the streets, in church they call "fellowship." You get together with your fellow brothers and sisters, coming together as a family to uplift one another.

There's no community without unity. We have to come united as one with like-minded people. When you're trying to rise up while hanging out with people going in a different direction, it's like the well-known 'crabs in a bucket' example.

Have you ever seen crabs in a bucket after being pulled from the ocean? They're scrambling to get out, but they keep pulling each other down. Every time one crab gets close to the top, another pulls it back down. None of them escape.

Faith Principles for Your Journey

Here are some crucial principles to remember:

- Without faith, it's impossible to please God (*see* Matthew 19:26 and Mark 10:27).
- With faith, all things are possible (*see* Mark 9:23).
- In your journey of recovery, all you need is faith the size of a mustard seed to move mountains (*see* Matthew 17:20).

Never give up on God because He surely won't give up on you. He is the author and perfecter of your faith (*see* Hebrews 12:2). That's why we need to speak to Him daily and hear from Him through His Word.

The Transformative Power

Faith is powerful because it changes you—your mindset, your vision, your purpose, your identity. You start to think outside of yourself and realize that your power doesn't come from you; it comes from Him.

"Faith isn't believing that God can; it's knowing that He will."
-Ben Stein[1]

Reflection Questions

1. How are you renewing your mind daily?
2. What areas of your life need God's strength instead of your own?
3. Who are the positive influences in your community supporting your faith journey?
4. What mountains in your life need to be moved through faith?
5. What are some ways your thinking has changed?

[1]Stein, Ben. "Ben Stein Quote." *FixQuotes*, 10 Mar. 2012, fixquotes.com/quotes/faith-is-not-believing-that-god-can-it-is-knowing-126067.htm. Accessed 24 Oct. 2025.

Action Steps

1. Go back and review your answer to Reflection Question #3. Intentionally contact people who have positively influenced you and express your gratitude through a phone call, message, or letter. Let them know how they have impacted your life.
2. If you are seeking additional mentorship, reach out to people you admire. Learning lessons from the study and work of others, through books, is also an impactful form of mentorship, and you can glean from people you may never meet.

Journal Space

_____

_____

_____

_____

_____

_____

_____

_____

Chapter 8: Building New Patterns

Moving Forward, Not Just Away

It would be incomplete for me to tell you what you shouldn't be doing and what you need to walk away from without sharing what you should be walking into. The whole purpose of this book is to help you overcome these disadvantages.

Creating New Routines

You have to create healthy routines and break out of the old ones. New habits. New desires. New thoughts. New goals.

Start by asking yourself:

- What kind of person do you want to see yourself become?
- What do you want people to say about you when they see you?

Your transformation can impact so many people—not just those alive right now, but even those who will come after you: your children and grandchildren. Every decision you make today can impact generations to come, if you would only understand that. We're so busy living for today that we forget to ask: *when tomorrow comes, are we ready?*

Setting Goals and Building Support

Start setting goals, write them down, take action steps, and build positive relationships. You need mentors. The Bible says there's safety in a multitude of counselors (*see* Proverbs 11:14). We need to surround ourselves with godly men and women (*see* Psalm 1) who will:

- Pour into us
- Teach us
- Guide us
- Pray with us
- Hold us accountable
- Strengthen us
- Challenge us

Developing Financial Responsibility

Take a course and learn how to handle money. Most of us who come from the hood and poverty weren't taught that. We don't understand how to manage money. Some may not even know how to build credit, open a credit card, or set up a bank account. Take a course. Learn.

The Power of Education

Education is key to developing yourself and being able to teach others. I'm not talking about college—I'm talking about reading books. Leaders are readers. Take courses. Always look to learn more.

If you want to:
- Be a non-profit leader, take a course on starting a non-profit.
- Open a business, take a business management course.
- Develop a skill, find training in that area.

Find what you're passionate about, what you're good at. You won't know unless you try different things and develop the skills and talents God has given you. Use them for His glory. Use them to build your story.

The Process of Growth

Take consistent progress through gradual baby steps. Be patient with yourself. Don't over-whelm yourself. Everything won't happen overnight. Change doesn't happen instantly. Blessings don't just come without hard work and necessary steps.

It starts with waking up, developing a prayer life, studying His Word, having a devotion, and/or learning to journal. Write your thoughts down, process them, take walks, meditate. All this contributes to your spiritual growth, healing, and personal development—your spiritual maturity.

Learning from the Right Sources

Surround yourself with people who are experts in whatever field you want to be in. Learn from them. Pick their brain. Do research. Take notes. Attend webinars and conferences. You won't learn much on the streets—I can tell you that.

It wasn't until I attended the right things and surrounded myself with the right people that I started to grow and learn things I should have learned years before. But I'm grateful I know them now. I now have a deep, passionate desire for education and studying.

Every year I make it a goal to take a new course. Even now, in 2025, I'm taking courses on Biblical counseling, apologetics, and leadership.

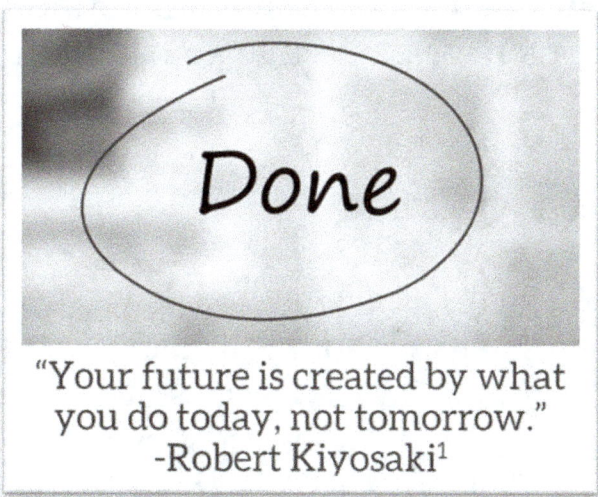

"Your future is created by what you do today, not tomorrow."
-Robert Kiyosaki[1]

[1]"Robert Kiyosaki Quote." A-Z Quotes, 2025, www.azquotes.com/quote/565110# google_vignette. Accessed 25 Oct. 2025.

I'm always trying to study something, whether God wants to use it to make me a more effective minister, a better leader, or just to help me communicate better with family and friends.

The Final Challenge

Build these patterns one brick at a time. Don't get discouraged. Don't let anyone tell you that you can't do things God said you can. Don't let your past hold you back or make excuses for yourself.

Remember this: If you don't build new patterns, you're guaranteed to go back to the old ones.

Reflection Questions

1. What specific routines do you need to establish in your daily life?
2. Who could serve as a mentor in the areas where you need growth?
3. What financial knowledge do you need to develop?

4. What skills or talents has God given you that you haven't fully developed?
5. How can you start building new patterns today?

Action Steps

1. Create a morning and evening routine to bookend your day.
2. Reach out to one potential mentor this week.
3. Look for a financial literacy course in your community or online.
4. Make a list of skills you'd like to develop.
5. Choose one new positive habit to practice daily for 30 days.

Journal Space

_____

_____

_____

_____

_____

_____

Dr. Pedro Rodriguez

Chapter 9: Restoration and Healing

The Journey of Healing

After breaking free and building new patterns, there's still important work to be done. The wounds of your past don't automatically disappear when you choose a new path. True transformation requires healing—the kind of deep restoration that mends what was broken in you.

Facing Your Trauma

Many of us from broken homes carry deep wounds we've never properly addressed:

- Abandonment issues from absent parents.
- Trust issues from broken promises.
- Identity confusion from lack of guidance.

- Emotional scars from verbal and physical abuse.
- Shame from our own mistakes and bad decisions.

These wounds don't heal by ignoring them. They need to be brought into the light, examined with honesty, and treated with care. In my case, I had to face the anger I felt toward my father for dying and leaving me, the resentment toward my mother for her addiction, and the shame of my own failures as a young father.

The Power of Forgiveness

One of the most powerful tools for healing is forgiveness. And it's often the hardest step to take. You may need to forgive:

- Parents who weren't there for you.
- Friends who betrayed you.
- Those who told you that you'd never amount to anything.

- The system that seemed stacked against you.
- Yourself for the choices you made.

Forgiveness doesn't mean what happened was okay. It means you're refusing to let that person or situation continue to have power over you. It's a declaration of freedom—freedom from the bitterness that can eat you alive from the inside.

Rebuilding Relationships

Part of healing involves rebuilding what was broken—especially relationships. This won't always be possible with everyone, but where it is possible, it's worth the effort:

- Reconnecting with family members.
- Making amends to those you've hurt.
- Building healthy new relationships.
- Learning how to be vulnerable in safe ways.
- Creating boundaries where necessary.

When I began my journey of healing, I had to learn how to be a better father to my daughters, how to be a faithful husband, and how to repair my relationship with my mother. None of this happened overnight, but each step brought more restoration.

Processing Grief and Loss

Many of us have experienced significant losses:

- Death of loved ones.
- Lost opportunities due to incarceration.
- Relationships that couldn't be saved.
- Dreams that had to be reimagined.
- Time that can't be reclaimed.

Grief is not weakness—it's a necessary part of healing. Allowing yourself to feel the pain of loss opens the door to eventual peace. For me, I had to properly grieve my father's death years after it happened because I'd never given myself permission to feel that pain.

Healing Your Self-Image

One of the deepest wounds many of us carry is a broken self-image. We've been told—or told ourselves—that we're:

- Not good enough.
- Destined for failure.
- Just another statistic.
- Defined by our mistakes.
- Unworthy of love and success.

Healing this requires replacing these lies with truth. God doesn't see you as a mistake or a failure. He sees you as His creation, with purpose and potential. Learning to see yourself through His eyes is a journey, but it's one that leads to true healing.

Creating Healthy Boundaries

Part of healing is learning to protect yourself from further harm through healthy boundaries:

- Limiting time with people who pull you back to old patterns.
- Being clear about what behaviors you will and won't accept.
- Learning to say "no" without guilt.
- Recognizing the difference between helping and enabling.
- Protecting your peace and progress.

I had to learn that some relationships, even family ones, needed boundaries if I was going to stay on my path of healing. This wasn't about rejection—it was about protection.

The Role of Professional Help

Sometimes, healing requires professional support:

- Counselors who understand trauma.
- Support groups of people on similar journeys.
- Pastors trained in spiritual guidance.
- Treatment programs for addiction issues.

- Mentors who've walked the path before you.

There's no shame in seeking help. In fact, it shows wisdom and courage to recognize when you need support beyond what friends and family can provide.

The Ongoing Journey

Healing isn't a destination—it's a journey. There will be:

- Days when old wounds feel fresh again.
- Moments when you slip back into old thought patterns.
- Situations that trigger memories you thought were healed.
- New challenges that reveal areas still needing attention

But with each cycle of healing, you grow stronger. The wounds may leave scars, but scars tell stories of survival and resilience.

"Healing doesn't mean the damage never existed. It means the damage no longer controls your life."
— Akshay Dubey[1]

Reflection Questions

1. What wounds from your past are still affecting your present?
2. Who do you need to forgive (including yourself) to move forward?
3. What relationships need restoration in your life?
4. Where do you need to establish stronger boundaries?
5. How has God already brought healing to parts of your story?

[1]https://spiritualgurugate.com/self-healing-quotes/

Action Steps

1. Write a letter of forgiveness (you don't have to send it).
2. Reach out to one person you need to make amends with.
3. Identify one professional resource that could help your healing process.
4. Start a healing journal to track your progress.
5. Create a list of truths to counter the lies you've believed about yourself.

Journal Space

_____

_____

_____

_____

_____

_____

_____

_____

_____

_____

_____

Dr. Pedro Rodriguez

Chapter 10: Your New Identity

Beyond Your Past

Throughout this book, we've walked through the journey from disadvantage to transformation. We've explored the lies that held us back, the patterns that trapped us, the empty pursuits that left us wanting, and the healing that restored us. Now, we arrive at the final destination: your new identity.

This isn't about putting on a mask or pretending to be someone you're not. It's about becoming who you were always meant to be—who God created you to be before the disadvantages, the lies, and the streets got their hands on you.

Children of God

The most fundamental shift in identity comes from understanding who you really are:

- Not a statistic, but a child of God.
- Not defined by your past, but by your Creator's purpose.
- Not limited by your mistakes, but empowered by grace.
- Not trapped in cycles, but set free for a mission.
- Not alone in your struggles, but part of a family.

When I truly understood that I was God's son—that He had claimed me despite everything I had done—it changed how I saw myself. I was no longer just a kid from Jersey City with a record. I was a man with divine purpose.

Purpose-Driven Life

Your new identity comes with purpose. You weren't saved just to escape destruction—you were saved for something:

- To share your story with others who need hope.

- To use your unique experiences to make a difference.
- To break generational cycles in your family.
- To rebuild what was torn down in your community.
- To reflect God's character in ways only you can.

For me, purpose came in the form of mentoring young men who were walking the same destructive paths I once traveled. Your purpose might look different, but it's no less significant.

Living as an Example

Part of your new identity includes being a living testimony:

- The power of transformation.
- The possibility of change.
- The potential that exists in everyone.
- The presence of hope in hopeless situations.
- The proof that statistics can be defied

When people look at your life, they should see evidence that yesterday's reality doesn't have to determine tomorrow's possibility. Your life becomes an argument against determinism and an advertisement for redemption.

Maintaining Your Progress

Your new identity requires maintenance:

- Daily renewal through prayer and God's Word.
- Regular accountability with trusted mentors.
- Continuous growth through learning and challenges.
- Intentional relationships that strengthen your foundation.
- Vigilance against old patterns trying to reassert themselves.

I've had to learn that my transformation isn't a one-time event but a daily choice. Each morning, I must decide again who I'm going to be and which voice I'm going to listen to.

Building a Legacy

Your new identity isn't just about you—it's about the impact you'll leave:

- The children who will have a different kind of parent than you had.
- The young people who will see a path forward because of your example.
- The community that will be stronger because of your contributions.
- The lives that will be changed because you were willing to change first.
- The story that will continue beyond your lifetime.

When I think about my daughters and now my grandchildren, I'm grateful they're experiencing a different kind of father and grandfather than I knew. The cycle is broken, and a new legacy is being written.

Embracing the Journey

Your identity will continue to evolve as you:

- Discover new gifts and talents.
- Take on new roles and responsibilities.
- Deepen your relationship with God.
- Overcome new challenges.
- Grow in wisdom and maturity.

This is the beauty of transformation—it's not static. You're not exchanging one fixed identity for another. You're embarking on a journey of becoming that will continue for the rest of your life.

Full Circle

Remember where we started in this book? With disadvantages and damage and hopelessness. Look at where we've arrived—at purpose and power and potential.

It would be dishonest to say the journey is easy. It's not. There will be setbacks. There will be days when old voices seem louder than new truths. There will be moments when you feel like you're sliding back into old patterns.

But here's what I know from my own journey: you are stronger than you think. God is more faithful than you can imagine. And the path forward, though difficult, leads to a life beyond what you dared to dream.

You are not defined by your disadvantage. You are not limited by your past. You are not destined to repeat cycles of destruction.

You are new. You are purposed. You are free. This is your new identity. Embrace it. Live it. Share it. You are not what happened to you. You are what you choose to become.

I am not what happened to me, I am what I choose to become. – Carl Jung[1]

[1]https://quotesoftheowl.com/i-am-not-what-happened-to-me-i-am-what-i-choose-to-become-carl-jung/

Reflection Questions

1. How do you introduce yourself now? Has your self-description changed?
2. What aspects of your new identity are still difficult to embrace?
3. What purpose do you believe God has for your specific journey and experiences?
4. How are you actively building a legacy different from what was passed to you?
5. Where do you see yourself five years from now if you continue on this path?

Action Steps

1. Write a personal mission statement based on your new identity.
2. Find one way to start mentoring or helping someone facing similar challenges.
3. Create a "legacy plan" with specific ways you want to impact future generations.
4. Develop a system for catching yourself when old identity patterns emerge.
5. Share your transformation story with someone who needs hope.

Journal Space

_____
_____
_____
_____
_____
_____
_____
_____
_____
_____
_____
_____
_____
_____
_____
_____
_____
_____
_____
_____
_____
_____
_____
_____
_____

Dr. Pedro Rodriguez

127

About the Author

Born in 1976 to teenage parents in Jersey City, New Jersey, I navigated the challenges of growing up in a rough neighborhood with limited resources. After losing my father at age 12 and watching my mother struggle with addiction, I faced the same choices many urban youth encounter today. By 16, I had dropped out of high school. By 19, I was a father to two daughters and facing adult charges.

But at age 21, an encounter with Christ transformed my life. Seven months later, I married my first daughter's mother, Gedy, and began a journey of restoration. Today, I serve as a church leader and mentor, dedicated to helping others find their way out of the same struggles I once faced. With three college degrees after being a high school dropout, I'm living proof that transformation is possible regardless of your starting point.

This book represents not just my story, but the possibility of transformation available to everyone willing to take the journey.

Dr. Pedro Rodriguez makes himself available for speaking engagements, mentorship and author events, small group workshops, and community events. Please email requests to Pedro@uyjinc.org.

Please visit the Urban Youth Justice website and find out more about our mentoring, life coaching, and life skills classes which are offered at no cost to youth due to generous donations from our supporters. Listen to our archived Voices of Truth podcasts and be encouraged by other inspirational content and find resources.

www.uyjinc.org

Resources

Crisis Support
- National Suicide Prevention Lifeline: 988 or 1-800-273-8255
- Crisis Text Line: Text HOME to 741741
- Substance Abuse and Mental Health Services Administration (SAMHSA): 1-800-662-4357

Faith-Based Support
- Local churches with youth programs
- Faith-based recovery programs
- Christian counseling services

Education & Career
- GED resources and preparation
- Community colleges with financial aid
- Vocational training programs
- Job readiness programs

Community Support
- Mentoring organizations
- Youth development programs
- After-school programs
- Community centers

Legal Resources
- Legal aid societies
- Reentry programs
- Expungement clinics
- Youth advocacy organizations

Family Support
- Family counseling services
- Parenting classes
- Child support services
- Family resource centers

Remember, reaching out for help is not a sign of weakness—it's a sign of strength and wisdom